ᴜNLY ONE IS REAL

Only One is Real

Reflections on Advaita and English Poetry

KENNETH VERITY

220 PUBLISHING

By the same author

Sonnets
Awareness Beyond Mind
Breathing with the Mind
The Spacious Mirror
The Unseen Reflection

First published 2007

ISBN 978-1-905479-02-3

Published by 220 Publishing
PO Box 220, Harrow, HA3 5SW

Printed in India by Thomson Press

CONTENTS

ACKNOWLEDGEMENTS

The central idea for this book arose from a lecture 'Advaita in English Poetry' given at the Nehru Centre (Indian Embassy) London, in May 2006, at the request of the Chetana Educational Trust (London).

I am indebted to my spiritual teachers Sri Shantanand Saraswati and Sri Nisargadatta Maharaj, from whom I have drawn instruction and profound spiritual sustenance.

I owe a debt of gratitude to Jim Whiting, my publisher, who commissioned this book, and Rodney Peel for their careful reading of the manuscript and for their helpful suggestions.

Lines from T S Eliot *Collected Poems 1909–1962* reprinted by permission of Faber and Faber Ltd. My thanks to Gavin Pomeroy for permission to reprint *At Night* and *The Bagman*; also to Norman Windsor for permission to reprint *A Trying Day in the Life of the Ego*.

Cover image (detail) by Cheng Yan
www.chengyan.net.

AUTHOR'S PREFACE

A foreign word like *advaita* does not at first glance seem to have any relevance to English poetry. The Sanskrit word (from an Asian language) means 'non-duality'. The duality in question could, in English, be described as God and Creation. In *advaita* philosophy the description might be 'the immanent conscious force (*Brahman*) is supremely One in the unity of creation, which expresses that one *Brahman*'. In English poetry as in all poetry, the substance is language, the essence is metaphor. It expresses *advaita* very well in universal ideas and principles.

Anglo Saxon (Old English) poets inadvertently made occasional allusions to *advaita* by referring to God as: 'One who all can' and 'He who frees the grain from wonder-lock' (ie enables the grain to be separated from the chaff). 'Thus Love's need is met'. It might be of interest to note that the Old English word *weird* means: 'to be; what is; things as they are' – truth? These lines from a series of gnomic verses appear in *The Exeter Book* – said to have been authorized by King Alfred (849–899).

Geoffrey Chaucer (1345–1400) spoke of *trouthe* (truth) as 'like to the light of the sun, enabling sight, constant and indistinguishable' (ie not partial or prejudiced). This concept seems to have accounted for the integrity of Chaucer's writings; he seems to have been stabilized in the universal self as he witnessed others of the human race.

Alfred Lord Tennyson (born in 1809) had, from early boyhood experienced a state of 'diminution of personal individuality and an expansion of himself into a universal unity of being'. He wrote of this to a friend, and the letter was read out (in India) before Sri Ramana Maharshi. He said: 'Ah! That is the state of abiding in the Self.' So the bearded old poet who wrote *The Charge of the Light Brigade* and *The Lady of Shallott* had long been experiencing an inner state of quietude, wholly fortuitously – apparently.

W B Yeats (born in 1865) (Nobel prizewinner) recovering from illness on Majorca, shared a convalescent home with Shankar Grajanan Purohit – later known to his disciples as Sri Purohit Swami. Together they produced a superb translation of *Ten Principal Upanishads*.

T S Eliot (born in 1888) (Nobel prizewinner) had a profound knowledge of the Indian Tradition and used Sanskrit words in his poetry.

It would be unrealistic to have expected English poets to have had direct contact with an *advaita* spiritual teacher. However, it is appropriate to mention the intense interest in Sanskrit and Indian literature that flourished in London and India towards the end of the 18th century. An eminent orientalist of this period was Sir William Jones (1746–1794). Barrister in London and later a judge in India, Jones published a *Persian Grammar*, Latin commentaries on Asiatic Poetry, a superb translation of the Sanskrit play *Shakuntala* and parts of the *Vedas*, and *Manu*.

A little later Friedrich Max-Muller (1823–1900) was hard at work with a massive output, including a *History of Sanskrit Literature (1859), Vedanta Philosophy* (1894) and he edited the extensive *Sacred Books of the East* series.

Whether or not other Victorian and Edwardian English poets were aware of all this it is impossible to say, but central ideas, universal principles and the unity of the Universe and its Creator, have appeared in English poetry down the centuries and many examples are given in this book.

Samuel Johnson the English poet and critic who lived until 1784 could, in spirit, have been writing in response to the *Rig Veda* and the *Bhagavad Gita* when he wrote:

> 'There, Poetry shall tune her sacred voice
> And wake from ignorance the Western
>   World.'

ADVAITA IN ENGLISH POETRY

Introduction

Several of the major formal religions which have arisen over the centuries, directed their loyalty to a supreme being which was and is, central to the understanding of their adherents. One meaning of our word 'religion' derives from the Latin *religare* 'to bind' so followers or adherents feel that they are held in their belief.

As a child I was consoled by the thought that God was a father figure, even if he was divine, and could be stern, and was all-seeing. Later, I discovered the *Upanishads* and Advaita Vedanta and at once the intellect in the brain-mind was attracted. The word *Brahman* was at first strange and not meaningful. Then I discovered that *Brahman* was a derivation by grammarians meaning 'origin' and 'expanding'. Researching the precise meaning of origin I discovered that Emerson when asked: What is originality? answered: 'It is being one's self.' Now here was a term I could live with – the 'self'. Pursuing understanding of the self as origin, a key *advaita* statement embodying this idea is: 'In the beginning was simply existence alone; One without a second.'

In the beginning would have been the very first moment. Yet here is a mystery. It is always the moment NOW. This is not time, it is eternity. Now is the ever present continuum. Just as the Sun seems to set when seen from Earth, so the moment will seem fleeting if mistakenly viewed in the context of time. A practical demonstration that would illustrate the difference between time and the eternal moment would be to put a lighted match to the wick of a candle, whereupon, the flame will consume the candle – its existence will elapse in time. If a bell is struck its brief sound will indicate NOW, no matter how often the bell is sounded again later. Whenever this happens, it will be NOW.

Wordsworth sees clearly the distinction between time (noisy years) and eternity (moments in the being). He seems to have discovered that the moment remembered (past) and the moment anticipated (future) are 'moments … in the eternal'.

> Our noisy years seem moments in the being
> Of the eternal silence: truths that wake,
> To perish never.
> *Intimations of Immortality*

The dictionary defines time as 'the serial elapsing of existence'. Time is a human invention derived for convenience in human affairs. The word 'time' means division. That which was divided was the day of 24 hours, as the spinning planet Earth turned in the light of the star we call Sun. As the Earth turned into its own shadow and darkness was experienced, two major divisions of time were available – Day and Night. These were not specific enough for pre-arranged meetings etc so 24 hours were further sub-divided until today, mankind has instruments that will measure a thousandth of a second. Samuel Pepys the diarist, (1633–1703), was Master of the Trinity House, President of the Royal Society, and Secretary to the Admiralty. He had the best pocket watch available in his day, but it was only accurate to within ONE HOUR! Consequently, appointments had to be made, for example, 'Between one and two of the clock'.

This has been explained in some detail because so many poets have alluded to passing time in contrast with the permanent, eternal moment now. As has been said: 'All poets are philosophers, but not all philosophers are poets.'

Shakespeare in the play *Macbeth* used the image of the burning candle to indicate the time duration of human life.

> Tomorrow, and tomorrow, and tomorrow,
> Creeps in this petty pace from day to day,
> To the last syllable of recorded time;
> And all our yesterdays have lighted fools
> The way to dusty death. Out, out, brief
>   candle!
> Life's but a walking shadow, a poor player
> That struts and frets his hour upon the stage,
> And then is heard no more;

After Macbeth's unhappy outburst about identification with 'time' we can remember that sounding a bell brings a reminder of the eternal NOW.

This 20th century poem, *At Night* by Gavin Pomeroy, indicates the vividness of perception that comes when the sense of time is suspended, and alertness registers exactly what is presented.

I don't know what the time is
  It is still dark.
The wind is boisterous outside
  And thrusting through cracks
Angry that it cannot find repose.
  The trees take the brunt
Of the night's wildness
  I can hear them tossing their heads.

Within, all is still, asleep.
  House square and unmoved
In mass and geometry secure
  Volumes tamed and at rest
Its stillness poised against
  The mellow tinkle in the drain
Of rain cheerily at work
  In its down to earth fashion.

The poem by Adyashanti which follows is addressed to 'existence', which is accorded the name 'Silence'. The feminine gender was linked by the Greeks to *Athene* the goddess of wisdom. The poet resonates with this general mythology of goddesses by an unspoken link with *Saraswati*, goddess of wisdom and knowledge, the mother of the Vedas.

The waves of mind
demand so much of Silence.
But She does not talk back
does not give answers nor arguments.
She is the hidden author of every thought
every feeling
every moment.

Silence.

She speaks only one word.
And that word is this very existence.
No name you give Her
touches Her
captures Her.
No understanding
can embrace Her.

Mind throws itself at Silence
demanding to be let in
But no mind can enter into
Her radiant darkness
Her pure and smiling
nothingness.

The mind hurls itself
into sacred questions.
But Silence remains
unmoved by the tantrums.
She asks only for nothing.

Nothing.

So what is the relevance of earthly time in the world to That which is eternal? Keats (1795–1821) would have us in no doubt:

> Stop and consider! Life is but a day;
> A fragile dewdrop on its perilous way...
> Time moves; eternity is still.

'Be still and know that I am God' is a Biblical injunction that directs us to that which is eternal in us (*Atman*) and its unity with *Brahman*.

It is in the unmoving stillness and silence of the present moment that *Brahman* is recognized and acknowledged. Here is how Wordsworth addresses the origin and expanding energy behind and within creation:

> Wisdom and Spirit of the universe!
> Thou Soul that art the Eternity of thought!
> That giv'st to forms and images a breath
> And everlasting motion!

For anyone who is not familiar with the essentials of Advaita Vedanta, I will briefly explain what it is and how it came about.

Early India

In the Indus Valley an indigenous civilization had flourished from about 2500 BC. This started slowly to disintegrate around 1500 BC, after invasions by Aryans, who arrived in successive waves through the mountain passes of the north-west. These early expansionist Aryans were semi-nomadic pastoral peoples, who brought with them a religion centred on scriptures called *Vedas*. The word *Veda* is a Sanskrit word meaning 'knowledge, sacred teachings'; these are Hinduism's oldest scriptures. The word *Hindu* (of Persian origin) was used by 12th century Muslim invaders of Northern India to describe the original population of Hind (India). *Hinduism* means 'the belief of the people of India'.

The invading Aryans had no system of writing but had brought with them from Iran a tradition of oral poetry and, from such evidence as the *Rig Veda* hymns, they seem to have taken particular delight in their language. This oral tradition, with its systems of memorization, ensured that when the *Vedas* came to be written down they were already established and complete. The Sanskrit language, in which early Hindu literature is written belongs to the Indo-European language-family and many Sanskrit words (in modified form) are found in Western languages.

In the later sections of the *Rig-Veda,* particularly the *Hymn of Creation,* there is a discerning probing and questioning into the cosmic essence behind the Created Universe.

Here is an extract from that Hymn, speaking of *Brahman* witnessing his creation.

> Then, what *is not*, was not; what *is*, was not:
>   The intervening divine motion of Creation
>   was not;
> That One breathed. Of a certainty, beyond
>   That was none other.
> That One, through light of knowledge,
>   brought Itself forth, to be.
> In the beginning, Self-delight, love and
>   desire evolved on That.
> By power of mind, the Poets penetrated the
>   heart, and found there the
> Bond of Truth in illusion.
> Who here truly knows? Who here could
>   proclaim whence *That* came
> into being, and from whence came *this*
>   detailed Self-expression?
> From whence came this detailed Self-
>   radiance, whether created or not?
> Only He in highest heaven, who is of this
>   the Witness,
> Is aware whether He knows or not.

Such a gnomic and esoteric utterance gives rise to questions:

> What is That which is beyond knowing?
> Being beyond human knowledge, how can
>   it be known?

Dualistic knowledge (influenced, as it must be, by subject-object perception and conditioning) affects natural intelligence which is rendered ineffective for proper discernment.

The Zen master would say: Go straight; don't know! This terseness needs unpacking. In essence it means 'seeing' without the concept. The 'direct way' is not usually practised in the West. Zen-like brevity is in English poetry. W H Davies, in four lines creates a graphic picture:

> Girls scream
> Boys shout
> Dogs bark
> School's out!

Followers of the *Vedic* religion had compiled its scriptures and established its religious practices by 800 BC; throughout the following two centuries it developed vigorously. The Greeks had regarded their poets as divinely inspired. Similarly, the earliest bards of the *Vedic* revelation had held a special place in the Aryan imagination, neither gods nor priests but *rishis* (hence *Maharishi*, 'great sage'), more powerful than either.

The visionary and poet, William Blake, emphasises the special importance of bards and seers for their greater understanding:

> Hear the voice of the Bard!
> Who present, past and future sees.

Between 600 and 500 BC, Indian society entered a period of fundamental transformation, and classical Hinduism gradually evolved to provide the spiritually structured life for most Indians during the next 2,000 years.

An important esoteric development occurred in Hinduism, which became known as *Jnanamarga*, or *The Way of Knowledge*. It evolved from the seeking by Hindu sages for special knowledge which would give mastery over the innermost questions of life. It was no less than the search for a key to the reality underlying the created universe, the single essence behind all diversity which pervades relativity. This supreme absolute, *Brahman* (defined as the Divine Ground of Existence) is, for Hindus, the impersonal Supreme Reality. The Way of Knowledge assumed its fullest expression in certain compositions of scripture called *Upanishads*. The word *Upanishad* means 'to sit down near to' the feet of the *guru* (teacher) to hear the full and final tuition of sages articulating the *Vedic* revelation.

The ultimate realization was that our real self is the unique metaphysical reality, characterized by consciousness. According to Hindu understanding the *Atman* (the real immortal self of human beings) is the non-participating witness which is beyond body and thought... The man of contemplation walks alone, seeing the *Atman* present in all things. It is his eternal satisfaction. As absolute consciousness it is identical with *Brahman*, the Reality behind the appearance. Because the *Atman* in the individual has total correspondence of identity with universal *Brahman*, its unique characteristics – eternal absolute being; absolute consciousness; and absolute bliss – are identical with those of *Brahman*. *Atman* is beyond concepts, but in this formulation of identical *Brahman* and *Atman*, two fundamental questions have converged: 'What is the Universe?' and 'What am I?' Implied in this is an immanent Presence which is ever existent and is one.

Hamlet, in Shakespeare's words, acknowledges a universal directing force:

> There's a divinity that shapes our ends,
> Rough-hew them how we will.

Here, Shakespeare echoes the Chinese sage Zhuangzi, who died in 285 BC:

> The universe and I exist together, and all
> things are one.

The *Upanishads* refer to the undivided and all-inclusive *Brahman* as *the* Reality, and the multiform world of experience as dreamlike unreality – phenomenal illusion (*jagat*). Because experience seems real enough to the senses, the question arises, how can there be two realities? Facing this intractable question with only the obscure brevity of the *Brahma Sutras* for reference, humanity needed an interpretative teacher to explain and offer a helpful commentary on obscure scriptures.

Adi Shankara – Master Teacher

At this juncture just such a master-teacher appeared – Adi Shankara or Shankaracharya (AD 788–820). His name means 'he who brings blessings'. Shankara was a philosopher, poet, scholar, mystic and reformer. Shankara's commentary on the *Brahma Sutra* (a work written presumably by a self-realized teacher) is an enquiry into the nature of *Brahman*, into the nature of the Self. Because so many Hindus were defecting to Buddhism, Shankara coupled his zealous reforms of Hinduism with a powerful attack on Buddhism. Despite his short life of 32 years, he composed numerous major works and founded a number of monasteries.

Shankara's great contribution to the spiritual life of the human race was to promote Advaita Vedanta (*advaita* means 'non-duality'). The word *Vedanta* means 'the end of the *Veda*', ie the complete knowledge of the *Vedas*. Advaita Vedanta reveals that the manifest Creation and the Ultimate Creative Principle are identical but distinct, (as the gold in a gold ring is independent of the ring). But it is important to recognize that creation is *totally dependent* upon the Creative Principle; the Creative Principle on the other hand, is independent and stands alone – it is Absolute. Modern particle-physicists have discovered that matter consists of continually moving fields of energy. Vedantic sages had already identified the finest level of that energy as, in reality, Consciousness. Human beings perceive the physical universe as *apparent* reality because they operate with the gross senses of the ego-limited body. Totally identified with the mind-body entity, each person considers it to be 'me' or 'myself'. With this point of view, the human mind superimposes upon real and unchanging consciousness an ever-changing manifest world of names and shapes, taking it to be the reality of existence.

To demonstrate this misconception, Shankara produced what has become one of his best-known teaching images – the metaphor of a piece of rope, mistaken in the semi-darkness for a snake. The misconception causes stress and fear but as soon as the rope is recognized to be rope, the mind is reassured and it does not convert it back into a snake. The mistaken view seems very real and the anxiety it produces is actual. *Advaita* explains that we, in our ignorance, continually impose the idea 'snake' (the manifest world) upon the 'rope' (*Brahman*). This quintessential teaching is expressed by Shankara in a single sentence: '*Brahman* alone is real, the world is appearance; the Self is nothing but *Brahman*.' The gold ring *is* gold.

Perhaps Robert Bridges (1844–1930) was aware of this universal idea when he wrote:

Awake, the land is scattered with light.

Plato in his *Timaeus* is close to the meaning of *Brahman* when he writes:

The origin of the universe contains within itself all intelligible things.

The expression *Self-realization* is often encountered in connection with Advaita Vedanta. It should be understood that, in this context, the word 'realized' does not mean 'to be made real' but rather 'to be experienced as the sole reality'.

To set Shankara in context chronologically within the early history of India, I have set out some important dates in the following chart:

INDIA	
Indus Valley Civilization, (Harappa and Mohenjo Daro)	c3000–1500 BC
Aryan invasion	1500 BC
Composition of Rig Veda	1500–900 BC
Upanishads; caste system established	1500–500 BC
Aryans in Indus River basin	1000 BC
Vedic religion established	800 BC
Development of Jainism	6th century BC
Gautama Buddha	563–483 BC
Darius invades Punjab	514–512 BC
Alexander the Great in India	327–325 BC
Emperor Ashok unifies most of India and actively promulgates Buddhist principles	274–237 BC

As for Shankara's dates (AD 788–820), there has always been great controversy among scholars. For my authority, I have taken the dates given by the renowned Indologist Professor A L Basham.

The only extant sculptured image thought to carry Shankara's likeness is a rather badly eroded sandstone relief from a South Indian temple. He is holding a *danda* or stick, which among many other meanings symbolizes the protection of *dharma*.

Dharma: Sanskrit word meaning: 'carrying, holding'. A comprehensive term referring to that essential quality which characterises our true essence; righteousness; the basis of human morality and ethics; the lawful order of the universe; the foundation of all religion. John Donne (who died in 1631) whose metaphysical poetry has some uncanny resonances with *advaita* ideas, wrote of *dharma*:

That All, which always is All everywhere

A softening of Donne's conciseness is found in the words of Sir Thomas Browne (1605–1682):

Nature is the art of God

Advaita Vedanta is one of the three systems of thought in Vedanta. Advaita Vedanta teaches that the manifest creation, the soul, and God are identical. This is because the manifestation is *saguna Brahman*, and soul is *jivatman* (*Brahman*), and God is *nirguna Brahman*. It is all *Brahman*, either with gunas or beyond (and therefore without) gunas (see page 32). As Shankara says in a Sanskrit verse: 'May the sentence explaining this proclaim the essence of a thousand books'. The sentence is:

> *Brahman* alone is real, the world is
>   appearance,
> the Self is nothing but *Brahman*.

A powerful and succinct statement of *advaita* was made by the Roman emperor Marcus Aurelius, one of the noblest figures in history. (He was born in 212 AD.) He wrote:

> One Universe made up of all things; and
>   one God in it all,
> and one principle of Being, and one Law,
>   one Reason shared
> by all thinking creatures, and one Truth.
>
> Meditations

He further added:

> All that is in tune with thee,
> O Universe, is in tune with me!
>
> Meditations

Centuries later, Alfred Lord Tennyson enables us to echo Aurelius with words from an English poet:

> One God, one law, one element,
> And one far-off divine event,
> To which the whole creation moves.
>
> In Memoriam: Conclusion

Superimposition

Shankara's celebrated metaphor of the piece of rope, mistaken for a snake in the semi-darkness, is not likely to make a strong impression on people who live in a temperate region like ours. I would just add, that when I did my National Service in Malaya, we always carefully checked our empty boots in case a thin black very poisonous snake was nestling inside! The projection of the snake on the rope as a mental mistake has, in philosophy, been given the formal name 'superimposition'. It means that something relative and unreal has been superimposed upon the underlying Reality – *Brahman*. In Sanskrit the word *Maya* is what the projecting power is called, and it gives rise to the illusions described by Shankara.

Human beings speak of 'sunrise' and 'sunset' as though the sun moved in an ascending and descending arc, through its zenith. This is *maya*. In fact, the spinning earth (which slightly tilts) turns into and out of, the light from the 'stationary' sun. The following is an example:

> *Ahampratyaya* is a modification in the mind that results in I-consciousness. It consists in the belief (*pratyaya*) that each of us is the body-mind, so mind employs the absolute consciousness to create thought projections, all associated with 'I' (*aham*).

Advaita Philosophy In The West

Advaita (a Sanskrit word) means: 'not two; non-duality'. In the Western World most of mankind practised religions and forms of worship where a dual state existed as the norm. A deity or powerful force, was worshipped by the supplicants, worshippers or followers. Only lone figures called 'mystics' seemed aware that the perceived duality was imagined, and that Oneness or Unity was how it really is. An example would be the unknown mediaeval mystic who wrote *The Cloud of Unknowing*.

If, in one major civilization like India, a section of its inhabitants had transcended the notion of 'duality' as a description of man's relationship with the 'Creator of the Universe', the question occurs: 'How did duality arise in the first place?' Primitive man observing comets, sun and moon eclipses, earthquakes and volcanoes, might well have thought: 'Some great power or force is *doing* all this'. Who or what is it? Imagination would get to work and a powerful being would be imagined. Napoleon said: 'Imagination rules the world'. Imagination is more than a visualization in the head, although that is the place where the activity occurs. In *Midsummer Night's Dream* Theseus, Duke of Athens says:

> Such tricks hath strong imagination,
> That, if it would but apprehend some joy,
> It comprehends some bringer of that joy:
> Or in the night, imagining some fear,
> How easy is a bush suppos'd a bear!

Then, for primitive man might come the thoughts: 'How can we mollify, placate, or 'win over' this supernatural power. Could we get 'him' on our side?' Can we pay 'protection money', divine hegemony, make sacrifices, take out a sort of 'divine insurance'? So human beings created a God who was the First Cause of all things and absolute Ruler of the World. Rituals and sacrifices could be devised. Special prayers could be uttered in specific rituals, which would be expected to be helpful and effective.

Superstition was widespread and it persists to the present day. In our culture, travellers finger their St Christopher trinket as the aeroplane takes off or tighten their grip on a lucky charm.

When there is an eclipse of the sun the Chinese have for centuries believed that the 'wicked sky dragon' is devouring the sun. By banging drums, saucepans, etc even in the 21st century (in London's Chinatown) they believe he is scared off. It appears to work; no eclipse of the sun has ever caused the sun's disappearance, so why stop now?

One device employed by mankind in attempts to influence the deity has been to sacrifice (Latin *sacrificare)* ie give up, surrender, suffer to be injured, destroyed, or lost, in order that something else may be gained. Over the centuries goats, sheep, oxen, people, even children, have been slaughtered.

It concerns many that a race as intelligent as the Greeks had a mythology full of sacrifices in attempts to influence or placate gods and goddesses.

To quote just one example:

> Agamemnon was wind-bound
> in the port of Aulis,
> together with the Greek fleet.
> He could obtain the return of
> favourable winds only by immolating
> to Artemis his own daughter, Iphigenia.
> But the goddess took pity on the innocent
> victim and snatched
> Iphigenia away at the moment of sacrifice.

Japanese who go to a Shinto temple to worship, have to ring a bell to let the deity know they are there. The deities of Heaven and Earth (*Kami*) and their spirits (*mitama*), which reside in the shrines where they are worshipped, seem to require some sort of signal or ritual using an external something (a bell) to alert the spirit.

In the Advaita Vedanta order of things, *Brahman* is expressed as Creation (*saguna Brahman*); it is eternally aware of itself as *Atman*, and no bell is required.

During the 17th century, in England, George Fox began to recognize that extreme obeisance and total duality diminished the self-esteem of mankind and seemed to bring into doubt the mercy and compassion of God. The Religious Society of Friends (Quakers) which he founded, have a beautifully neutral compassionate saying: 'There is that of God in everyone'.

Some two thousand years before the Quakers, advaitins would determine how the Creator of All and Everything could be expressed without duality, in the unity of the one universal existence.

Tennyson once said:

> If I could understand a flower, root and all, I would have understood the whole existence.

A person without this *advaita* comprehension has been described in a poem by Peter Bell:

> A primrose by a river's brim
> A yellow primrose was to him,
> And it was nothing more.

Walter de la Mare is the author of sensitive, imaginative lyrics in traditional form. He was an accomplished poet, storyteller and essayist. The following verse begins what has been a favourite poem for generations of children:

> *The Listeners*
> 'Is there anybody there?' said the Traveller,
>   Knocking on the moonlit door;
> And his horse in the silence champed the
>   grasses
>   Of the forest's ferny floor.
> And a bird flew up out of the turret,
>   Above the Traveller's head;
> And he smote upon the door a second time;
>   'Is there anybody there' he said.
>
> 'Tell them I came, and no one answered,
>   That I kept my word,' he said.

There is an elegant simplicity in this curious poem. Like an allegory it has several layers of meaning. A suggested *advaita* interpretation follows:

The male 'traveller' is in duality seeking something outside himself. He is in 'the forest' a symbol for obscurity and loss of bearings. The traveller's horse (like *manas* or discursive mind) as soon as momentum ceases, is attracted to 'something to eat'.

A bird flew up 'above the traveller's head'. Above the head; having the head severed, (*Sir Gawain and the Green Knight*) suggest that 'the head' will not be the means to 'go through the moonlit door'. Moonlight is the reflected light of the sun.

The traveller knocks, expecting a response from beyond the door. He knocks – perhaps expecting admittance. He asks again: 'Is anybody there?'

He thinks that what he seeks is outside himself, behind one of the many doors: religions, faiths, systems, therapies …

He came and no outside help met his need. 'Tell them I came … I kept my word' he said.

Advaita Vedanta would suggest He *was* what he *sought,* but none of *The Listeners* responded. The traveller speaks; the Listeners only listen. They are integral with witnessing Awareness in *advaita*.

> If you cannot find truth where you are,
> where else do you expect to find it?
> *Zen saying*

Some Basic Points of Advaita

Advaita Philosophy teaches the following essentials: for the normal human being 'I-AM-ness' is the consciousness, without which, one would not know that one exists. Consciousness requires a physical form. At conception, the mother's and father's bodies (the products of the essence of food) start the process for the birth of another individual body. Once born, this brain-mind-body, the 'individual', will develop a seemingly separate distinctive personality. During its birth–to–death life there will be the sense that 'I am the doer.' During its dream-like existence, events will 'happen' to this dream-like 'doer'. A total transformation of these circumstances can only come about when the identification with the individual body is dissolved into the knowledge 'I AM'. But the knowledge 'I AM' is subject to the three *gunas (gunah)*. The whole creation is pervaded by three forces or energies. Their Sanskrit names are *rajas* (activity); *tamas* (inertia); and *sattva* (harmony). When the concept 'I AM' is no longer present, I AM is no longer subject to the three *gunas*; it becomes *nirguna* and merges with Reality (the Source). This is the universal Self – what one really is.

When the human being is totally orientated towards the happenings coming in from the world, with no semblance of an inner ground, or inner sense of identity, this might well manifest in a bizarre figure like the man observed by the poet Gavin Pomeroy in 1991:

The Bag Man
He got on the bus
His hat was yellow,
Waterproof and pinned
With different coloured badges
One said, "Where's Wally?"

His beard was hoary
And his greyed hair stuck out
And straggled his collar.

Sleeves were turned back
To adjust the tailored raincoat
Now hardly fitting
To his tenancy;
And permanent occupation
Had made its brown, soiled and shiny.

His plastic bag, red handled
Said, "The cat's out of the bag"
Which his margarine containers
And motley threatened to follow.

He sat on the outside seat
By a tall trim girl
And cockily chatted her up
But she knew where to get off.

So alone again and little wonder
For his other badges said
"You're not the first I've had

And you won't be the last"
and
"I'll show you mine
If you show me yours".
Then I got off.

The wise see even *The Bag Man* as an embodiment of the Self, however enveloped. In contrast here is how Hamlet the philosopher prince glimpsed Man and his developed potential:

> What a piece of work is a man! How noble
> in reason! How infinite in faculty! in form,
> in moving, how express and admirable! In
> action, how like an angel! in apprehension,
> how like a god! the beauty of the world!
> the paragon of animals!

Shakespeare's reference to man as 'the paragon of animals' worries some people. But in Persia, among the Sufis, a man who had not become one with universal love, was considered to be merely 'a talking animal!' However, it should be remembered, that simply to exist safely in the physical world the 'human animal' has developed evolutionary selectivity for that purpose. The dog has an incredibly developed olfactory sense and can detect through smell minute traces of a substance, and by smell can anticipate an immanent seizure or disabling episode in their human owner's health. An eagle can discern a rabbit 5 kms (3 miles) distant. Our senses could be said to be 'just right' for our ordinary natural existence. The criticism of the human situation by *advaita* teachers is that we may limit our understanding by too much emphasis on 'gross senses' and the ego influence.

Shakespeare, in *Measure for Measure* refers to:

> The wanton stings and motion of the sense.
> *Act I, scene iv*

In one line from *The Tempest* he speaks of the superimposition of the changing on the unchanging as 'this insubstantial pageant':

> We are such stuff
> As dreams are made on, and our little life
> Is rounded with a sleep.

A poem by Swami Rama Tirtha begins:

> You are the Lord of the Universe
> And you have made yourself a beggar.
> You are the creator of time,
> And you have made yourself time's pawn.

In W B Yeats's translation of the *Katha Upanishad* we find:

> One who knows that the senses belong not
>   to spirit, but
> to the elements that are born and die,
>   grieves no more.

The Human Brain-Mind

As is stated elsewhere in this volume, the primary function of the brain is to optimize the individual's response to the personal environment.

Millennia before the Western knowledge of Neurology, Neuro-physiology, etc was known to mankind, the Arabs and the Hindus had reflectively monitored and analysed (as far as their knowledge allowed) the functioning of what we now term the Brain-Mind, Psychology, and Psychiatry.

The Hindu sages presented a useful but (by contemporary medical knowledge) a rather simplistic description of the brain-mind and central nervous system.

The whole brain-mind and central nervous system, as an entity, is termed the *antahkarana* – the inner instrument. With overlapping and mixing of function, the early Hindu system is sub-divided into four:

Buddhi:	perception, intellect, discernment, discrimination, intelligence, intuition, all drawing upon the consciousness of the atman.
Ahankara:	the 'I'-maker, self-consciousness, sense of I-Me-Mine.
Manas:	attention, volition, determination, will, capacity of thought.
Chitta:	thinking and reasoning, emotional evaluation.

This short volume of *advaita* in English poetry does not contain the space to unfold the majesty and complexity of the brain-mind functioning, nor the brain chemistry; nor the hormonal chemistry which makes a major contribution to our emotional responses, but a few basic essentials are as follows:

Only an organism that moves from place to place requires a brain. An organism that stays still responds automatically to changes in its environment. Plants often have sophisticated reactions, eg sunflowers rotate their flower-head to face the sun, but they do not need to move across the ground, so they possess no brain.

The human brain is the product of gradual evolution and adaption to changing conditions over hundreds of millions of years. The human body is assembled from more than 50,000 billion cells of at least 200 main kinds. The brain has 100 billion *neurons* (brain cells). Each of us has a brain divided into two major sections or hemispheres. The two halves of the *cerebrum* and *cerebral cortex* are joined by an organic 'cable' (the *corpus callosum*) containing some 300 million nerve fibres. The brain-cells (*neurons*) in the cerebral cortex are connected by 100,000 billion links (*synapses*). This detail and complexity is a fascinating study and a basis for admiration of *Brahman* and Its expression in the evolutionary selection process.

Ordinarily there is a duality which is accepted as the natural condition:

1. The inner model in the brain-mind which mirrors the so-called external world. Many people respond and react by taking their predominant perception from their 'inner world'.

2. The outer, or so-called 'real' world, presents its data to the sense perceptions of the brain-mind. This seems to have been the prime 'intention' behind evolutionary selection which has produced the contemporary human being. The metaphor the 'Gateway of the Senses' is sometimes employed to 'link' the duality of the inner and outer worlds.

The *advaita* of oneness points to the human experience being one existential adventure, sensed and known in the immediacy of the eternal moment Now. It is blissful to dwell in the only moment – no past, no future – just a moment-to-moment immediacy.

Shelley offers a sound reason for being in the moment now; otherwise, he says:

> We look before and after;
> We pine for what is not

In passing, perhaps mention should be made of the careless way people refer to 'hearts and minds' in such clichés as: 'It's a question of how to win over hearts and minds on this issue'. The expression 'hearts and minds' is a kind of shorthand for ideas with their associated feelings. The ideas are prompted by a wide range of attitudes and pre-judices, including self-preservation and religion. These stem from the intellect.

The word 'feeling' from the Old and Middle English *felan,* means: 'to have physical sensation of'. When undergoing stress people say: 'my heart missed a beat'; 'my heart leapt into my mouth'; 'my heart sank'. Under stress, the heart rhythm changes as blood circulation is intensified. The pumping organ can be felt thumping in the chest, and there-fore has (over millennia) been discerned as 'the seat of the emotions'. The release of *adrenalin, norepine-phrine, endorphins,* and other hormonal chemistry, ensures that emotional intensity is strong. To call all this 'the heart' is convenient, but the Advaita Vedanta teaching means so much more when this 'hinterland' is known about.

The aspect of feeling is often overlooked in its application to *advaita* practice. When we part from friends and loved ones, we ask them to 'keep in touch'. This usually implies, simply, communica-tion. However, with the subtle sense of touch and full awareness, it is possible to extend this and be 'at one' with the environment, and even beyond, to the universe. Enlarging this, if the duality and sepa-ration commonly experienced was felt intensively, there would be a deep urge to move towards unity.

A Chinese saying from 80 BC said:

> 'The capacity of the mind is as great as that of space; it is infinite'.

The God Concept

A major difficulty of understanding when investigating spiritual psychology is how to regard or understand the origin and primal force of the Created Universe. Any concept of a creator becomes an identity as a noun. The noun is then made a 'proper noun' (a name). Soon, anthropomorphic attributes are generated and projected by mankind. 'God', or whatever the deity is considered to be, acquires human form and human characteristics. Attributions of human thoughts and feelings are superimposed on the original 'thought' or 'idea'. In the past various safeguards and precautions were tried. God has no name; It/He has an unpronounceable name; or a name that must never be uttered. 'It' 'God' is a spirit, is invisible, is all-pervading, all-seeing, omnipotent, yet it is the Lord or the Father. By contrast, the *advaita* term: *Brahman* meaning 'origin' and 'expanding' seems simpler – even scientific.

> From thee, great God, we spring, to thee we tend,
> Path, motive, guide, original, and end.
> *Samuel Johnson, The Rambler*

> We are because God is.
> *Swedenborg Divine Providence*

If *Brahman* is regarded as 'God' by an advaitin (follower of *advaita* teaching), what could he expect to learn about the nature of Brahman? The word 'nature' from Middle English and Latin, *natura*: means 'nature of things' and 'order of things'. This indicates that we are considering the deity *in* creation ie *saguna Brahman*.

> Honour Him, Honour Him
> The revealed God.
> *(Chinese, date unknown)*

Shelley, as a poet, reaches all parameters of the natural world as he speaks of *Brahman* and his Creation:

> He is made one with Nature: there is heard
> His voice in all her music, from the moan
> Of thunder, to the song of night's sweet bird
>   (nightingale)

The teaching of *advaita* principles in English translation usually deals with the question: what is the nature of the Absolute or the nature of the Ultimate Creative Principle of the Universe (Absolute, Brahman, Self, God) which is presented as a three-fold oneness?

This is satchidananda (*saccidananda*) a compound word, one translation of which is: unbroken existence; absolute consciousness; desireless bliss.

Interpretation

Because we see and perceive everything from a 'point of view', we therefore feel individual and believe ourselves to be separate observers. Once this concept of separation has been established and the idea of 'person' derived, there follows 'my view of things' and 'my interpretation'.

Brain and mind process the data available to 'our perception'. With this, we do the best we can to make sense of what we see around us. We learn how others have responded previously to similar impressions; we formulate questions; we seek answers. Many turn to religion, philosophy – and poetry – for responses to these questions.

That which poetry represents, it expresses in language. In skilled hands, an impression – even hard fact – may be conveyed distinctively by figurative language. A simple fact may be designated in scientific writings by an unembellished noun, but in poetry, directness and clarity are not enough. By use of a metaphor or a figure of speech the same fact is alluded to with grace and feeling. But what is this 'fact' upon which so much literary ability may be lavished?

Nietzsche (1844–1900) believed (many would think rightly) that 'There are no facts, only interpretation.' Turning from observed things to the inner world: 'All thinking is interpretation,' wrote Susan Sontag (1989). So if the 'facts' of our everyday world are an interpretation of our sensations, and if thinking about those facts is more interpretation, are we not erecting one intellectual meaning upon another? It is perhaps for this reason that poetry (which can carry reason, insight, and feeling) seems to go straight to the essential meaning of things.

The verb 'interpret' comes from the Latin *interpretari*, 'to explain, expound; translate'. It is thought to have originally meant, 'to act as agent between two parties in a bargain'. There are other meanings:

1 to translate into a foreign language as interpreter

2 to represent objectively so as to bring out meaning and character – as a musician interprets the music of a composer

3 to understand in a specific way, or construe a meaning – as when a person's silence is interpreted unfavourably

A psychologist might define 'interpretation' as 'an activity in which a physical or psychological datum is related to a datum'. In other words, what is 'out there' – the world – is related to what is 'in here' – the head. Interpretation is a way of understanding, a view of a set of facts from a certain perspective. Some argue that it is the interpretation that matters rather than the facts themselves.

To take a simple everyday example: hardly a look or gesture passes between two human beings without it being interpreted for significance and meaning. The exchanges between a pair of servants from the two rival Houses in *Romeo and Juliet* go like this:

Abr   Do you bite your thumb at us, sir?

Sam   I do bite my thumb, sir.

Abr   Do you bite your thumb at us, sir?

Sam   (Aside to Gregory) Is the law of our side if I say ay?

Greg (Aside to Sampson) No.

Sam   No, sir, I do not bite my thumb at you, sir; but I bite my thumb, sir.

Act I, scene i

Each of us in our daily exchanges with others interprets and evaluates frowns, smiles, words, etc. We construe for significance or implication.

Self

Our word 'self' was present in Old English and Middle English. It meant: 'one's own individual personality, and identity, as distinct from those of others'. As though reaching for something deeper, the dictionary offers: 'one's own individual interests, advantage; the essential quality, character, genius, quintessence, inmost nature of anything'. The range of comprehensiveness in the dictionary meanings indicates that 'self' is not easy to define. The human being combines universality and unique individuality.

Every physically embodied human being has been constructed using an almost unique coded 'script'. This is its DNA (deoxyribonucleic acid) which has designed each specific individual person. This DNA coded sequence defines the physical self and is what our immune system recognizes as 'self'. The immune system is a natural innate security arrangement; a protection against invasion by a 'germ', ie a pathogenic micro-organism alien to the blood stream, not conforming to the DNA blueprint, and therefore 'not self'. Whereupon the pathogen is destroyed by special cells (*macrophages* and *phagocytes* etc). All this applies to the physical self. There is however a 'mental self' which also contributes to our identity.

At birth each human being is provided with the universal mental architecture – the brain. As happenings occur and are experienced, the brain becomes personalized as 'the mind'. The function of the brain is to optimize the individual's response to the environment. An important feature of the brain-mind is the ego. The 'ego' is that portion of the psyche which possesses consciousness, maintains its identity, and recognizes and tests 'reality'. This carries the sense of self, mentally.

For a Psychologist the undifferentiated predispositions, traits, and tendencies, awaiting realization in the coded script of the double helix of DNA (in conjunction with experience of life) constitute the most subtle layer of personality. In *advaita* this coded script is the Causal Body.

The psyche derives from the Greek, meaning the 'organ of thought and judgement'. In Medicine today the psyche is defined as: 'The human faculty for thought, judgement, and emotion; the mental life, including both conscious and unconscious processes.' The physical self and the mental self, together with the senses, offer the protection we call 'life preservation' or 'self preservation'.

A question arises: 'How does all this become the focus we call self'? Every living creature has self. Consider something as simple as an acorn. The acorn with its DNA has within it the 'blueprint' for a fully mature oaktree. If the acorn is left in a dry corner of the house it will remain an acorn indefinitely. Whereas, push the acorn into damp soil and in a few weeks a root will emerge at one end and a leaf or two at the other. The acorn is potential; the growing tree is fulfilment. So what triggered dormancy or quiescence to move into activity?

In philosophy this mysterious process is the point where the Self (with a capital S), manifesting as the life-force, activates the acorn's realization as oaktree. The parallel equivalent can be read across the Creation, from the human being down to the greenfly.

It is perhaps obvious that not only is the acorn (with its DNA) the dynamic which produces the mature tree, but it acts as an attracting focus for the natural forces in the acorn's environment - sunlight, air, rainfall, as well as all the nutrients and chemistry in the surrounding soil. The 15 ton mature oak tree is constructed from the materiality of the natural surroundings. How like the situation for a human being. In this instance, the self with its DNA atttracts nourishment for the body, impressions, stimuli, perceived possibilities etc.

The Self is that part of us which remains free of the everyday concerns of the personality (lesser self) yet which seems to guide and support our volitional, purposeful advance 'forwards'. In the *Upanishads* of Indian philosophy we are reminded of the unity of Self and God (*Brahman*).

Extracts from the *Eesha Upanishad*, based on a translation by Sir William Jones (1746-1794):

> Whatever exists in this universe
> Is to be regarded as within the One,
> As if wrapped in a vesture.
> Man, renounce the world and do not
> Covet that One's property.

May you engage in worldly acts without
Loss of knowing that unity.
There is one only Being who exists
Unmoved, yet moving more swiftly than
 mind,
Outstripping the senses, although like gods
They strive to reach Him. Who like air
Supports all vital action. He is within
Yet outside this universe. Beholds all
Living creatures within Himself the
 Universal Spirit,
and regards none in contempt.
That man who understands this perceives
Unity of being and has no illusion.
He, the all-pervading brilliance, is without
 body.
All wise, above all beings, the Self-existent.

Of interest here is our word 'individual'. The
term 'individual' from Middle English means:

1. Indivisible as a complete entity.
2. Inseparable from a greater whole.

The embodied *Atman* seems very individual on
both these counts.

Knowing nothing of *advaita* terms (apparently)
Shakespeare - 'master of our sweet English tongue'
– speaks of the individual in contradistinction to
the supreme Self:

but, for my single self,
I had as lief not be, as live to be
In awe of such a thing as myself.

Esther Dyson (1951-99) speaks of selfhood in activity rather than in stillness. She says:

I think of who I am
As what I've done.

Cyril Connolly (1944) has recognized that separation from the One Self is condemnation to a confining cell of isolation.

We are all serving a life sentence
in the dungeon of self.

In the following short poem that still, silent place beyond name and form is described in a mystical way:

Meet here, where you want nothing,
and where you are nothing;
The here that is unspeakable.
Where we meet only mystery to mystery,
or we don't meet at all.
Meet here where you find yourself
by not finding yourself.
In this place where quietness is deafening,
and the stillness moves too fast to catch it.

Adyashanti.

Soul

Over the centuries mankind's idea of 'soul' has undergone many changes. It is evident from Frazer's researches (*Golden Bough* etc) that savages thought that a man had several souls. In Greek civilization notably in Homer, there are several words which mean something like 'soul' and seem to refer to parts of a man that have different functions. (See the English dictionary meanings later in this section).

Alexander Pope (1688–1744) had rather a secular view of the contents of a soul:

> It is with narrow-souled people as with
> narrow-necked bottles: the less they have
> in them, the more noise they make in
> pouring it out.

Shakespeare, in *The Merchant of Venice*, defines 'soul' as:

The immortal spirit which inhabits the body and is the cause of life and sense.

Wordsworth (1770–1850) – in his *Intimations of Immortality* – wrote this:

> Thou, whose exterior semblance doth belie
> Thy Souls' immensity;
> Thou best Philosopher, who yet does keep
> Thy heritage, thou eye among the blind.
>
> Thanks to the human heart by which we
> live,

Thanks to its tenderness, its joys, and fears,
To me the meanest flower that blows can
  give
Thoughts that so often lie too deep for tears.

Wordsworth contributes more thoughts on his soul:

Fair seed-time had my soul, and
I grew up,
Fostered alike by beauty and by fear.

Alexander Pope alludes to the soul in association with certain functions of the human being which equip us to practise Advaita Vedanta teaching:

To wake the soul by tender strokes of art,
To raise the genius, and to mend the heart;
To make mankind, in conscious virtue bold,
Live o'er each scene, and be what they
  behold:
For this the Tragic Muse first trod the stage.

Matthew Arnold (1822–88) British poet and critic, speaks of some of our uncertainties (including those concerning the soul):

We cannot kindle when we will
The fire which in the heart resides,
the spirit bloweth and is still,
In mystery our soul abides.

Our word Soul was present in Old English (Anglo Saxon) as *sawol*. A good dictionary offers the following meanings:

> The non-material part in man which thinks and wills; the personal entity of an individual regarded as separate and separable from the body and distinguishing him from others; psychologically the inner activity of which one is directly conscious; the vital mental principle without which consciousness either totally or partially ceases; the ethical or emotional nature of man, as contrasted with his bodily, or intellectual powers and desires; that which expresses the essential part of anything; quality, property which gives life and energy to anything; a departed disembodied spirit.

This rather comprehensive body of meaning certainly seems to contain the essence of a human being. As we are exploring Advaita Vedanta it is important to see what the Indian philosopher would mean by 'soul'. A good source is the fine book by Monier Williams *Indian Wisdom* (published in 1875). Monier Williams proposes as the common faith of educated Hindus what he calls 'rationalistic Brahmanism'.

This looks upon soul as of two kinds:

a) supreme Soul (*Paramatman, Brahman*, etc),

b) the personal individuated soul of living beings (*jivatman)*

This Teaching avers that the personal soul of every human being, like the supreme Soul, has existed everlastingly and will never cease to exist.

Shakespeare in just one play, *Hamlet*, uses the word 'soul' 38 times and in several of the ways included in the foregoing dictionary definitions: These words are from Act 1:

> … but, as this temple waxes,
> The inward service of the mind and soul
> Grows wide withal.

> The friends thou hast, and their adoption tried,
> Grapple them to thy soul with hoops of steel;

> When the blood burns, how prodigal the soul
> Lends the tongue vows:

> and we fools of nature
> So horridly to shake our disposition
> With thoughts beyond the reaches of our souls.

Ego

Ego from the Latin means 'I'. That part of the individual which thinks consciously.

In Psychoanalytic Psychology, the ego is that part of the psychic apparatus which is the mediator between the person and the reality (the world). Its prime function is the perception of 'reality' and adaptation to it. Subsidiary 'tasks' include perception, (including self-perception and self-awareness); motor control (volitional action); use of anxiety mechanism to ensure safety and self-preservation; the memory.

Some religious teachers insist that the ego should be 'got rid of' or eliminated. The ego is the creature's sense of itself in relation to its environment. An amoeba, a tiger, a mouse, all have this sense which motivates behaviour towards life-preservation, indeed, self-preservation. This is often misunderstood. Spiritual teachers want us to avoid confusion between the ego sense of 'I AM' and 'That of God in everyone' termed *Atman*.

In Philosophy, the Self is that part of us which remains 'above' the everyday concerns of the personality, yet which somehow seems to steer us and be a support when needed. In *advaita* terms this situation evidences the *Atman* – the immanent conscious force *Brahman* – and *buddhi,* the faculty of discernment and distinction. This does not make us 'special'. To be special is to be very limited. In the supermarket or shop, a 'special price' or 'special offer' never lasts; they are always temporary.

The knowledge 'I AM' is the 'film' of the individual's life, the destiny. The DNA and immune system both help to determine the destiny. As the brain-mind absorbs experience and is conditioned by influences and the happenings of our environment, we believe in the identified embodiment. We think 'this is who I AM'.

The child receives early instruction from its mother: 'We are parents, you are child. This is how you should behave'. After the child is two or three years old it gradually gets involved in 'I' and 'mine' and it gradually loses the joy that 'I AM'. Later, instructions are given by teachers, lecturers, and other outside influences. Concepts are formed, attitudes arise, ideas are embedded. With our concepts safely stored and mistaken for knowledge, we think this is who I AM.

Advaita Philosophy avers that we should become concept-free. Eliminate concepts like the concept 'I AM'. Even the concept 'I am waking up' is the basis of illusion.

In *advaita* terms, sleep and waking are misnomers because we are simply dreaming. The ego dreams it is awake.

For reflective men and women the question arises: What am I, or Who am I? A good system of mind-stilling meditation will dissolve spurious answers. When 'I am' arises, the world and everything else appears; when 'I am' subsides, everything subsides.

Amazingly, we have projected onto our sense of ourselves a world of our own imagination. It is based on memories, desires, and fears; and we are imprisoned within it. To be aware of this is to break the spell and become free. It is the *tamas* of the ego that holds us prisoner. Here is a poem by the English poet Norman Windsor (1994), which describes how the ego works:

> *A Trying Day In The Life Of The Ego*
> Trying to know something
> Trying to do something
> Trying to be something
> Trying to change something
> Trying to get something
> Trying to have something
> Trying to avoid something
> Trying not to avoid something
> Trying.

One practical exercise suggested by *advaita* teaching is to 'view life as a play'. This is to cultivate detachment and avoid becoming embroiled in the minutiae of everyday events. Shakespeare reminds us of the universal play:

> All the world's a stage
> And all the men and women merely players;
> They have their exits and their entrances;
> And one man in his time plays many parts,
> His acts being seven ages.

Person

Our word 'person' (Latin *persona*) means 'character, part, role'. The Etruscan *phersu* means: 'masked figures'. The theatre was, and still is, the place where an actor dons a mask. In Greece, China, Japan, a male actor could present a female figure; become a monkey or a dragon; become a god! In the role, the mask confers the status. In ordinary life, many professionals 'dress for the part' as we say. Artists and photographers may grow a beard; the Harley Street consultant often wears 'morning-dress'.

Advaita teaching emphasizes the importance of witnessing the play without losing the true identity. We undertake many roles in life: parent, boss, employee, tutor, student, etc, but beware of limitation through habit or custom. Here is a story emphasizing this:

> In a small town in India, a merchant owned a sweet-shop. He was diligent and his trading was scrupulously fair. One day, an entrepreneur arrived in the town intending to set up a small supermarket there. He noticed the shopkeeper, and was impressed with his principled approach to trading. He decided to put him in charge of his new superstore. He put his generous proposal to the small trader with a beaming smile. The shopkeeper frowned, shook his head in refusal and said: 'It's not possible; who would look after my sweetshop?

Spirit

The word *spirit* occurs in Middle English. In Latin the word *spiritus* translates into English usage as: 'breath; breeze; breath of life; life; soul; mind; spirit; energy; courage; pride; arrogance'. Among a wide range of statements using the word 'spirit', there is even *'the Holy Spirit'*, the third Person of the Trinity. (Some people cannot now accept Holy Ghost). Spirit also alludes to any powerful distilled alcoholic drink. In some areas of philosophy and psychology there are allusions to 'pursuing the spiritual path'. A typical result is the discovery that your 'I–am–ness' is the state 'to be'.

The Self or Spirit referred to by poets as a presence is drawn into experience by their words. Here is a description of this presence and its effect in *Lines Composed A Few Miles Above Tintern Abbey* by Wordsworth:

> … And I have felt
> A presence that disturbs me with the joy
> Of elevated thoughts; a sense sublime
> Of something far more deeply interfused,
> Whose dwelling is the light of setting suns,
> And the round ocean and the living air,
> And the blue sky, and in the mind of man;
> A motion and a spirit, that impels
> All thinking things, all objects of all
>   thought,
> And rolls through all things.

The *Spirit presence* mentioned by Wordsworth is synonymous with the Self alluded to by Tennyson:

> The spirit of poetry is the Self or, put
>   another way,
> it is the Spirit pervading all creation.

A concluding word on this vast subject is given by W B Yeats who, in collaboration with Sri Purohit Swami, put into English an Indian spiritual teaching, the *Eesha Upanishad:*

> The Self is everywhere, without a body,
>   without a shape, whole,
> wise, all knowing, far shining, self-depend-
>   ing, all transcending.

In the continuum which is poetry, words are always available to express what has been vouchsafed to the poet in the mirror of imagination.

Genius

Each of us has the usual mental architecture, but from the moment of birth, experience began which was unique to us, yet was general in its features. We were each of us endowed with genius.

As a word, 'genius', from the Latin and Greek means principally: 'The tutelary god or attendant spirit allotted to every person at birth'. In the 17th century, in this country, genius had come to mean: 'Natural ability, quality of mind, natural aptitude'. But, it includes reference to creativity. It also means: 'Native intellectual power of an exalted type; extraordinary capacity for imaginative creation, original thought, invention, or discovery'. So how is the inborn genius to be released? The first step is to realize that your genius is the innate spirit present since birth.

Genius is innate, we are all born with potential for expressing that genius, but few do. Shakespeare was a boy born in a Warwickshire market town. His father and mother are thought to have been able to read, but not write. Einstein's brain was examined minutely after his death to see if his genius was explicable by some unusual physical characteristic, but there were none. These two men, with Isaac Newton and many others, were born with the universal mental architecture, but it was how they used their brains that made the difference.

The word 'genius' includes the definition: 'extraordinary capacity for imaginative creation'. What about the word 'extraordinary'. From the

Latin, *extra ordinem,* our word means 'outside (the usual) order'. So what is inhibiting the release of our genius? In the fairy story of Aladdin (*Alla-addin*) and his wonderful lamp, the lamp was rubbed or polished and the geni or *jin* emerged. It was ready to do the bidding of the owner of the lamp. The historic Buddha on his deathbed said to his disciples, 'Be ye lamps unto yourselves.' Robert Browning, the English poet, in his *Paracelsus* seems to mirror the words of Buddha:

> Truth is within ourselves: it takes no rise
> From outward things, what e'er you may
>   believe.
> There is an inmost centre in us all,
> Where truth abides in fulness.

As the celebrated Hindu maxim says:

> *Atman atmana pashya:* ' Know thyself by
>   thyself'.

Meditation

Integral with the *advaita* tradition is the process of meditation. Indeed, it has been said that when the Absolute meditates, it manifests Creation. There are many levels of meditation. The Sanskrit word *dhyana* means 'concentration' but meditation means so much more than the focus of mind and spirit.

Man has discovered what he truly is and inwardly hears the authentic universal voice, only when the obscuring ego is reduced in intensity. This process is often achieved by one or other of the meditation techniques available over the centuries. Here is Tennyson describing just such a process:

> More than once when I
> Sat all alone, revolving in myself,
> The mortal limit of the Self was loosed,
> And passed into the nameless, as a cloud
>   melts into heaven.
>
> *The Ancient Sage*

In his poem *Ash-Wednesday*, T S Eliot says:

> Teach us to care and not to care
> Teach us to sit still.

In two lines Eliot indicates loving commitment, renunciation, and meditation.

What is meditation? It is commonly understood to be full attention on one thing. Other thoughts are kept away during the process. The single thought must disappear eventually to leave thought-free consciousness. This has been described as existence witnessing itself, or consciousness witnessing itself. After a period of elapsing awareness of existence, the physical-mental embodiment makes itself evident again. Here in two sonnets, some impression is given of meditation and emergence from meditation. Remember, all this is offered in words but the ineffable is beyond words.

I sit in meditation – thought has ceased;
The growing silence deepens under will;
Discursive mental pressures are released
And mind is centred, wide awake and still.
Inner responses cease their constant play
As each disturbance yields to will's fine
  force;
All trace of movement gently ebbs away
As what is cognate turns towards its source.
Direction lies beyond what is unknown,
The darkness is translucent clear and full;
Subject and object disappear in one;
Being is fully present, and is all.
  At this, experience recedes in rest
  And what I knew, no more is manifest.

Coming out of meditation is not quite the reverse of entering meditation, but of course there is a deep state of refreshment afterwards.

Emerging from Meditation

When like a deep cool lake the mind is still,
Yet to the inward eye as space is seen,
Life waits awhile; but then that space must
   fill.
Attention cannot stay thus held serene.
From non-cognition, mind again must
   know;
The outer and the inner now are two;
Attention's point is caught and tempted out,
The world of things and forms is back in
   view.
Mind joins again with ears and labels
   sounds,
The eye sees forms and mind gives each its
   name;
Distinctions now are drawn, so too are
   bounds,
All's difference now which then was all the
   same.
   In unity the many parts are one;
   When mind is still, diversity is none.

These and four other sonnets on meditation were written by the author of this book some thirty years ago. The 'process' of meditating refines with practice. It now seems like Existence witnessing itself or Consciousness witnessing itself.

A Zen Buddhist monk meditates:

> Sitting on a small
> Black cushion facing the wall –
> Letting go of 'my' world.
> *Kenneth Verity, Awareness Beyond Mind*

NOTE: Just sitting (*zazen*) allows the mind to empty of thoughts, such as the 'me-concept' and attachment to 'I-me-mine'. The freedom is delicious, although at the time the 'experiencer' is absent.

In the context of Advaita Vedanta mention should perhaps be made of *nirvana* which from the Sanskrit means: 'a blowing out; extinguished'. In Buddhism (which originated in India and once was beginning to supersede Brahmanism) it has a specific meaning:

> A state of complete blessedness attained
> when the individual soul is absorbed into,
> and united with, the divine infinity, and
> all personality is extinguished. This can
> occur during a well developed system of
> meditation.

Love

The *sufi* (Persian mystic) and the realized man of Advaita Vedanta teach that the universe manifests through love, is sustained and nourished by love and, ultimately, it will dissolve into love. Love is that which dissolves separation. It therefore is the integrating and unifying force in creation maintaining its unity. Even magnetism and gravity are unifying and integrating forces within seeming separation. Natural forces (like volcanoes and earthquakes) merely re-arrange the name and form of matter within the unity of creation.

Mind ponders on the force of gravity,
That constant pull towards the centre point;
Mass drawing mass in strange affinity,
Attracting by a mystery conjoint.
Since light has mass this law pervades it
  through,
Curving its earthward path from outer space,
Veiling what lies beyond eternal blue,
Keeping obscure creation's distant face.
But Nature's laws are everywhere the same
When from a cosmic standpoint they are
  seen,
And mind discovers in this lawful frame
How matter is concealed within form's
  screen.
  Thus gravity presents a vital fact;
  All that exists must closely interact.

Kenneth Verity, Sonnets

The concept 'love' is *prema* in the Sanskrit language. The word 'love' in the Old English, means 'connected with'. The Sanskrit *lubh* means to desire and the Latin *lubet* 'it pleases'. These three etymological roots carry elements of the phenomenon ordinarily thought of as 'love'. The English poet Chatterton writes:

> What is love? 'tis nature's treasure,
> 'Tis the storehouse of her joys;
> 'Tis the highest heaven of pleasure
> 'Tis a bliss that never cloys.

The concept 'free' is embodied in the English language with love. The benign phase of a human loving relationship demonstrates this with the true lover wanting to free the beloved from the lover's own expectations and desires. The lover desires only to give everything, including the self (ego). There is much to do with surrender here.

The whole spectrum of physicality, intellect, and the emotions is spanned by the human expression of love. Love has a vital spiritual dimension. Its operation is central to the continuing evolution of consciousness in mankind. Indeed, for many, love defines the growing point of human development. That point is the centre which is everywhere, excluding nothing but including everything.

On love, no personal limitation can be placed, it being a universal. It is an unmeasured giving of the self, as exemplified in *Romeo and Juliet*:

Juliet: My bounty is as boundless as the sea,
         My love as deep; the more I give to thee,
         The more I have, for both are infinite.
                              Act II, scene ii

It is usual for an aesthetic dimension to inform the perception of the lover towards the beloved, particularly early in the relationship. This is not an over-estimation; rather a response to the essential self in the other, innocently seen:

Romeo: O! She doth teach the torches to
         burn bright.
         It seems she hangs upon the cheek
         of night
         Like a rich jewel in an Ethiop's ear;
         Beauty too rich for use, for earth
         too dear!
                              Act I, scene v.

Because Love is that which dissolves separation, man can gain self-control and can afford to interact freely with sense objects. To be free, he must constantly remember the Truth – I am an expression of That origin and expansion, *Brahman*.

Immediacy

Because (as *advaita* philosophy teaches) experience of creation is dream-like, the ordinary human being seems to operate on 'auto-pilot'. In contrast, when an individual is responding to creation by moving with awareness in the context of stillness, certain qualities of experience are evident: Immediacy, spontaneity, directness, stillness, oneness.

The eternal in poetry intersects the everyday and awakens the dreaming human being who believes himself to be awake. The substance of poetry is language; its essence is metaphor. The metaphor deepens meaning but can seem at first to obscure meaning. This knowledge can help us to 'see' the Self everywhere. It is necessary to see with the eye of discernment, the 'Wisdom Eye' (also known as the Third Eye). The Self is, as it were, screened by the creation, but even an older child knows that the parent is holding the 'treat' behind their back. The Self is everywhere; always look at significance, not name and form (*nama-rupa*).

In moments of stillness, which seem outside time, ordinary things seem to take on a deeper significance, and the immanent Reality of the Absolute seems much closer. Following are two examples from English poetry.

Edward Thomas (1878–1917) captures a moment that reveals the stillness which is always present when he was in a steam train that made an unscheduled stop in Oxfordshire. It is called *Adlestrop*.

Yes, I remember Adlestrop –
The name, because one afternoon
Of heat the express-train drew up there
Unwontedly. It was late June.

The steam hissed. Someone cleared his
  throat.
No one left and no one came
On the bare platform. What I saw
Was Adlestrop – only the name.

And willows, willow-herb, and grass,
And meadows sweet, and haycocks dry,
No whit less still and lonely fair
Than the high cloudlets in the sky.

And for that minute a blackbird sang
Close by, and round him, mistier,
Farther and farther, all the birds
Of Oxfordshire and Gloucestershire.

When time is dissolved in stillness, its eternal quality can make the moment seem endless.

In the following extract from a poem by Rupert Brooke (1887–1915) he reports what he saw when time appeared to be at rest. Everything that takes place in this poem occurs between the start of tea being poured into a cup, and the point where the cup is filled!

Dining-room Tea

I watched the quivering lamplight fall
On plate and flowers and pouring tea
And cup and cloth; and they and we
Flung all the dancing moments by
With jest and glitter.

Till suddenly, and otherwhence,
I looked upon your innocence
For lifted clear and still and strange
From the dark woven flow of change
Under a vast and starless sky
I saw the immortal moment lie.

I saw the marble cup; the tea,
Hung on the air, an amber stream;
I saw the fire's unglittering gleam,
The painted flame, the frozen smoke.

For suddenly, and otherwhence,
I looked on your magnificence.
I saw the stillness and the light,

Freed from the mask of transiency,
Triumphant in eternity,
Immote, immortal.

Dazed at length
Human eyes grew, mortal strength
Wearied; and Time began to creep.
Change closed about me like a sleep.
Light glinted on the eyes I loved.
The cup was filled.

Habitually we see the amazing, varied and often beautiful screen of transient forms of ephemeral objects, but we miss the underlying unchanging Reality. The immanent reality which is always present is called *Sat* in the Sanskrit language. It is the existence which was in the beginning and is now.

As T S Eliot said in *Four Quartets*: We have the experience but missed the meaning. He added: For most of us, there is only the unattended moment.

Our experience is that to which we choose to give attention; the rest passes us by!

It is Absolute

In ordinary speaking we say: It is raining; it is growing late; it is interesting; it is all a matter of right understanding. What is this 'It'? Who or what is this unspecified noun? There isn't anybody *doing* all this, so what is the universal It? An answer is offered by James Broughton and Joel Andrews:

> This is It
> and I am It
> and You are It
> and so is That
> and He is It
> and She is It
> and It is It
> and That is That.

There must be a big universal VERB at work in Creation. In the West we have a teaching statement (with Greek origins)

In the Beginning was the Word.

A question this raises is whether this word is a noun or a verb.

Hamlet says: 'To be or not to be' – that is, shall this manifest in existence or not? To bring this short discussion to a close we have to decide: Is GOD a *noun*, a *verb* or both – or something else? *Brahman* means 'origin' and 'expanding'; this is both a noun and a process.

A change of viewpoint is usually a first step towards a systematic alteration in thinking. This can lead to a transformed inner being, capable of expressing the unity of *advaita*. Without transformation, merely learning about the teaching cannot dispel duality.

English poets deal with all possibilities as they express their understanding of creation and its possible origin.

Wordsworth glimpsed a woman that attracted him, and whether by choice or inadvertence kept his distance by viewing her with a philosophical insight:

> And now I see with eye serene
> The very pulse of the machine;
> A being breathing thoughtful breath,
> A traveller between life and death.
> *She was a Phantom of delight*

Wittgenstein said, famously, in his *Tractatus Logico-Philosophicus* (1922): 'The limits of my language mean the limits of my world!' He also said:

> 'What can be said at all can be said clearly; and
> whereof one cannot speak whereof one must be silent.'

Wittgenstein was brilliant, but a poet will not accept his words lightly.

The master teachers of Advaita Vedanta say: When all is understood, words are not necessary. The Zen buddhist prefers practicality over words. In Zen, it is said that the use of words is like scratching one's shoe because the foot itches.

A modern poet, who died recently, Thom Gunn (1929–2004) was aware that the light in each of us seems to be surrounded by a fog of attachment, holding us to our own viewpoint, our sense of who we think we are – to the limitations of our individuality. Attachment takes many forms. Einstein who stressed the importance of his insatiable curiosity said: 'The only thing that interferes with my learning is my education.' For many, education is the acquisition of concepts which we then tend to stay attached to.

Each human being is born with the same universal mental architecture, but after birth each person's experience personalizes the brain and it becomes the individual mind. It has been said that our brain-mind identifies us, making us who we are. Thus the universal Self acquires limitations. If we dropped the concept 'self' we could naturally 'be the Self'.

The so-called 'personality', the conditioned ego, can interpret 'what is' (truth) in bizarre ways:

> They said, 'You have a blue guitar,
> You do not play things as they are.'
> The man replied, 'Things as they are
> Are changed upon a blue guitar.'
> *Wallace Stevens (1879–1955)*

Here are two verses from Thom Gunn's poem *Human Condition*, in which his evening walk through enveloping fog prompts a philosophical reflection on the separation and isolation we experience with the concepts 'I, me, and mine':

> The street lamps, visible
> Drop no light on the ground,
> But press beams painfully
> In a yard of fog around.
> I am condemned to be
> An individual.

> Much is unknowable.
> No problem shall be faced
> Until the problem is;
> I, born to fog, to waste,
> Walk through hypothesis,
> An individual.

The poet has discovered and expressed in a Western way, something about personal attachment (the 'I, me and mine' attitude) that seems to hold us a prisoner to our desires.

Speaking of our attachments, T S Eliot in *The Waste Land said:*

> What are the roots that clutch, what
> branches grow out of this stony rubbish?

Now see how T S Eliot expresses this idea, speaking as one who is held in time; distracted by the indecisions of what might have been, but who finally comes to rest in the *Atman*. It is an extract from *Burnt Norton*, one of his Four Quartets:

Time present and time past
Are both perhaps present in time future,
And time future contained in time past.
If all time is eternally present
All time is unredeemable.
What might have been is an abstraction
Remaining a perpetual possibility
Only in a world of speculation.
What might have been and what has been
Point to one end, which is always present.

Go, said the bird, for the leaves were full of
  children,
Hidden excitedly, containing laughter.
Go, go, go, said the bird: human kind
Cannot bear very much reality.
Time past and time future
What might have been and what has been
Point to one end, which is always present.

The Self never undergoes change; the intellect never possesses consciousness. But when someone sees all this world, he is deluded into thinking 'I am the seer, I am the knower'.

William Wordsworth in his poem *Intimations of Immortality* looks behind the ever moving *jagat*, the created universe, to the origin of man. He describes the innocent wonder of the baby in its growing up:

> There was a time when meadow, grove, and
>   stream,
> The earth, and every common sight,
> To me did seem
> Apparelled in celestial light.

Wordsworth, as a child, savoured and enjoyed the innocence and wonder of childhood, without the ego claiming and marring the experience. He penned the amazing line: The Child is father of the Man.

A further line catches Wordsworth's awareness of the unity of the *Atman* and the embodiment of brain-mind and body: 'By our own spirits we are deified'.

> Our birth is but a sleep and a forgetting:
> The Soul that rises with us, our life's Star,
>   Hath had elsewhere its setting,
>   And cometh from afar:
>   Not in entire forgetfulness,
>   And not in utter nakedness,

But trailing clouds of glory do we come
  From God, who is our home:
Heaven lies about us in our infancy!
Shades of the prison-house begin to close
  Upon the growing Boy.

The Greeks when they were to perform some creative act dedicated their activity to the muse who was patron, overseer, and inspirer of their art form. This process removed the sense of personal doing from the one who was to produce the composition, painting, sculpture etc. The muse channelled the power of Apollo by inspiration. Inspiration means: 'to be breathed through' by the divine power.

Apollo: The God of the sun and patron of truth, archers, music, poetry, medicine, and prophecy. His oracle in Delphi was an order of prophets who gave advice to Greece. Apollo had a retinue of nine Muses one for each of nine different art forms:

Calliope	*Terpsichore*
Clio	*Euterpe*
Thalia	*Melpomene*
Erato	*Polyhymnia*
Urania	

Three earlier muses were:

Melete (Meditation)
Mneme (Remembrance)
and *Aoede* (Song)

The two muses of Poetry were:

Calliope: Muse of epic or heroic poetry and
              of poetic inspiration and eloquence.
Erato: Muse of erotic poetry.

The Tenth muse was a name given originally to the celebrated female poet Sappho, but Shakespeare leaves us to infer who is the tenth muse.

Sarasvati: The goddess's name (derived from a legendary river) was held sacred by the people of India, even in Vedic times. Sarasvati, as a goddess, later became *Brahma's* consort. (Very like Apollo and his retinue of nine muses.)

Sarasvati is the goddess (muse) of the 'stream of speech', of rhetoric, scholarship, and intuition (the divine word). Sanskrit and its alphabet (*Devanagari*) is attributed to her. She is also the patron of the arts, especially music.

Shakespeare dedicated his writing activity to the Muse. He referred at one point to the tenth Muse (transcending the classical nine of the Greeks). Could the tenth Muse be the supreme being or self which may be inferred (like *Brahman*) as *nirguna* beyond the limiting attributes of manifestation in creation?

All such dedications, whether by Greeks, Shakespeare, or religious devotees, are made to acknowledge a power beyond our ordinary selves. This effectively lifts us above personal limitations, and any sense that we have to perform the action personally. Here is the Shakespeare sonnet referring to the tenth Muse; it is number 38:

How can my Muse want subject to invent,
Whilst thou dost breathe, that pour'st into
  my verse
Thine own sweet argument, too excellent
For every vulgar paper to rehearse?
O! give thyself the thanks, if aught in me
Worthy perusal stand against thy sight;
For who's so dumb that cannot write to
  thee,
When thou thyself dost give invention light?
Be thou the tenth Muse, ten times more in
  worth
Than those old nine which rimers invocate;
And he that calls on thee, let him bring
  forth
Eternal numbers to outlive long date.
  If my slight Muse do please these curious
  days,
  The pain be mine, but thine shall be the
  praise.

The way imagination works is that our senses
seem to cohere as we focus on an object, and the
object is then experienced as 'other than myself'.
This separation is reinforced by the way human
beings view the world we live in.

(See Interpretation, pages 42–44)

Nature's Elements

When the early philosophers of India perceived the world imaginatively, it was entirely represented by certain component elements: aether, air, fire, water and earth.

In this scheme the many separate 'things' are grouped in a unity of substance and kind. All the elements are present in any object. Take a glass tumbler for instance. The clear transparent glass is earth. The silica or sand was taken out of the ground and melted with fire, made molten and moulded or formed into this shape and then cooled. The 'fire' in your eye enables you to see its shape. Water, as moisture in the air, hugs its surface. Air fills the space (aether) within the glass.

Suppose I fill the glass with drinking water from a jug. What happens to the space in the glass? The water displaces the air which is driven out, but it occupies the space which remains there. We can fill the space but it doesn't go anywhere.

There are many references to the elements in English poetry (which with the three *gunah* constitute creation.) Here is each one of the five elements expressed in poetry. First, a line from an English sonnet praising Monteverdi, who was known in his lifetime as *Divino Claudio!*:

> Cremona's noblest son, your skills caress
> The aether into audibility!
>
> *Kenneth Verity, Sonnets*

Next, here is a reference to superimposition, as expressed by Shakespeare (in *The Tempest*) as he mentions the element 'air':

> These our actors,
> As I foretold you, were all spirits and
> Are melted into air, into thin air.

16th century poet Edmund Spenser spoke of:

> World-mothering air,
> Nestling me everywhere.

All fire in the world comes from the star we call 'sun' and Shakespeare in his play *Hamlet* refers to the redness of fire in the sunrise:

> But, look, the morn in russet mantle clad,
> Walks o'er the dew of yon high eastern hill.

All water on the earth arrives in various ways from the seas and oceans, and Wordsworth links, metaphorically, meditation and the element water.

> Hence in a season of calm weather
>   Though inland far we be
> Our souls have sight of that immortal sea
>   Which brought us hither.

Rudyard Kipling speaks of the element earth in just four lines which include both a wide spectrum, and the narrowness of human attachment:

God gives all men all earth to love,
   But since man's heart is small,
Man finds one spot which then shall prove
   Beloved over all.

John Hall Wheelock wrote a poem called *Earth*: here are four lines from it:

Grasshopper, your fairy song
And my poem alike belong
To the dark and silent earth
From which all poetry has birth.

The differentiation of Nature casts its shadow on the unity of seeming two. The unity of all and everything is differentiated by the brain–mind, as it strives to understand.

William Wordsworth attempts to put into words the balancing stillness that occurs when stillness dissolves the outer and inner into one. He speaks of excellence, pure function and best power; the seen and the seeing. He seems to be describing the *advaita* witnessing awareness.

A balance, an enobling interchange of action
   from without and from within;
The excellence, pure function, and best
   power
Both of the object seen, and eye that sees.
The Prelude

As an aid to detachment from I-me-mine, *advaita* teaching urges each of us to 'Witness life as a play or drama.' W B Yeats sensed the preliminary stage of this important approach to witnessing: 'We begin to live when we have conceived life as a play'.

When the sun is directly above an object, no shadow is cast. The shadow appears when we are looking from a particular angle instead of seeing directly.

Unless the drama is witnessed in conscious detachment we may well find ourselves echoing the words of T S Eliot in *The Rock*:

> Where is the life we have lost in living?
> Where is the wisdom we have lost in
>   knowledge?
> Where is the knowledge we have lost in
>   information?

How can this have happened? Eliot tells us:

> Between the idea
> And the reality,
> Between the motion
> And the act,
> Falls the Shadow,
>   *The Hollow Men (1925)*

Eliot intrigues us with his arcane reference to 'the shadow'. Several possible meanings can be inferred from a piece of poetry.

Here is Kathleen Raine's poem, *Shadow*:

> Because I see these mountains they are
>   brought low,
> Because I drink these waters they are bitter,
> Because I tread these black rocks they are
>   barren,
> Because I have found these islands they are
>   lost;
> Upon seal and seabird dreaming their inno-
>   cent world
> My shadow has fallen.

In terms of Advaita Vedanta that shadow is the belief that we are the birth-to-death embodiment. A celebrated children's couplet says:

> I have a little shadow that goes in and out
>   with me,
> But what can be the use of him is more
>   than I can see.

William Blake (1757–1827) glimpsed the same reality in *Auguries of Innocence*:

> To see a world in a grain of sand,
> And heaven in a wild flower,
> Hold infinity in the palm of your hand,
> And eternity in an hour.

Knowledge of ideal beauty is not to be acquired. It is born with us. Innate understanding is born in the man; it is truly himself. Blake said:

> 'The man who never in his mind and
> thoughts travelled to heaven is no artist.'

Catherine, Blake's wife, was a patient and devoted companion who accepted her husband's visions with equanimity. On one occasion she said, 'I spend very little time in Mr Blake's company; he is usually in Paradise!'

Ananda K. Coomaraswamy (1877–1947) considered the poem, like the icon, to be a support for contemplation, linked to the inner life of the person. The poet objectifies and discloses his feeling, allowing it to be shared by others.

It is of the essence of poetry to question by what process the external becomes the agent's expression. Attempting to define visual imagination Eliot cites *Macbeth,* observing that it offers not only 'something to the eye, but, so to speak, to the common sense':

> Light thickens, and the crow
> Makes wing to the rooky wood.
> *Act III, scene ii*

Wordsworth responded to the question 'What is a poet?' Here is what he said:

He is a man speaking to men: albeit a man, it is true, endued with more than ordinary lively sensibility, more enthusiasm and tenderness, who has a greater knowledge of human nature, and a more comprehensive soul, than is common among mankind; a man content with his own passions and volitions, one who rejoices more than other men in the spirit of life that is in him; and delighting to contemplate similar volitions and passions seen in the divine expressions of the Universe.

Wordsworth said of poetry:

Poetry is the breath and finer spirit of all knowledge. Poetry flows from an emotional recollection having its origin in tranquillity.

This same poet hints at *Brahman's* presence in creation (although, of course, he would not use the word *Brahman*). Here are some thoughts from his *Lines composed above Tintern Abbey*:

We are laid asleep
In body and become a living soul:
While with an eye made quiet by the power
Of harmony, and the deep power of joy,
We see into the life of things.

Wordsworth makes it clear that he regards a temporary disengagement from his immersion in fleeting, tiring wordly activity, as a benign refuge:

> When from our better selves we have too
>   long
> Been parted by the hurrying world, – and
>   droop;
> Sick of its business, of its pleasures tired,
> How gracious, how benign is solitude.
>   *The Prelude*

Perhaps a formal meditative technique would have transformed Wordsworth's solitude into something deeper.

Interludes of peace in the continuum are important for maintaining a serene equilibrium, but an old Persian adage warns us not to be too sensitive to wordly pressures:

> If you are irritated by every rub, how will
>   your mirror be polished?

Consciousness

Our word 'conscious' derives from the Latin *conscius* 'knowing, aware of'. Man is a conscious being. Consciousness is the most obvious and most mysterious feature of the human mind. Each of us is quite aware that we are the subject of experience; that we receive sensations of pleasure and discomfort; we have perceptions, we think, we have ideas; but quite what consciousness is puzzles neurologists and scientists. We are conscious of *the inside* of our being, and we are aware of *the outside* of ourselves.

When many Westerners are interpreting Advaita Vedanta teaching they translate the mysterious pervasive presence and influence of *Brahman* (whether within creation or beyond creation) as 'consciousness'. The foremost advaitins such as Sri Nisargadatta Maharaj, are very clear that consciousness is in creation and requires a form in which to manifest. Beyond creation, and prior to consciousness, is Witnessing Awareness.

> Awakening to
> The awareness beyond mind –
> Only now is real.
>
> *Shinri (1931–)*

Attention (metaphorically) 'should' be always on the SOURCE, ie 'seeing' without the veiling concept of *maya*. Consciousness 'brings trouble' because it is within creation. Witnessing awareness is beyond creation – not subject to birth and death.

Before man was born the consciousness was not present; after his death the consciousness will not be present – it comes and goes. It conditions everything – concepts, ideas, hopes, and all things. Awareness is always beyond consciousness – it is prior to consciousness. If awareness is there, that is where the consciousness appears. To put it very simplistically, *nirguna* is awareness; *saguna* is consciousness.

Now (in life) the body is here; it is made of elements. The awareness exists prior to the elements. The moment that the consciousness of 'I' appears there is the experience of the world, of suffering and happiness. Suffering and happiness are happening in the consciousness, but awareness does not know the duality of suffering and happiness.

Meister Eckhart, the 13th century German mystic seemed to understand the mirror-effect of witnessing:

> The eye with which I see God is the
> same eye with which God sees me.

Florence Nightingale (1820–1910) described Mysticism as the attempt to draw near to God, not by rites or ceremonies, but by inward disposition. Heaven is neither a place nor a time. Einstein the scientist said:

> The most beautiful thing we can experience
>   is the mysterious.

Witnessing

The word 'witness' that we use today was in Old English (Anglo-Saxon) and Middle English as *witnes(s)*. The word is 'Wit and 'ness'. In Old English, *witan* meant 'to know'. In Old English and Middle English, *witt* meant 'mind, intelligence'. The words 'witnessing awareness' as the 'I know' beyond creation, apply to *Brahman* – the origin of, and the expanding expression (as Itself) into Creation. *Nirguna Brahman* with *saguna Brahman*, not two, but one – *Advaita*.

Poetry can be confined in dimension or it can express the universal. In the church of Saint John Baptist, Burford, Oxfordshire is the monument to Sir Lawrence Tanfield, who died in 1625. He was a lawyer of the Elizabethan and Tudor Age who rose to be Lord Chief Baron of His Majesty's Court of Exchequer. When he died, his widow composed a poem which was engraved on the family monument. It uses the words shadow and wit with their earlier emphasis and meaning:

Here shadowe lie,
  Whilst life is sadd.
Still hopes to die,
  To him she hadd.
In bliss is he
  Whom I lov'd best;
Thrice happy shee
  With him to rest.

So shall I be
  With him I loved;
And hee with mee
  And both us blessed.
Love made me Poet,
  And this I writt;
My harte did doe yt
  And not my witt.

When the personal observer becomes witnessing, each of us is enabled to be true to our own Self.

You cannot love 'others' as yourself, unless you have realized that each one of us is the embodied *Atman* and 'others' are as one with yourself. We will neither pretend to be what we are not, nor deny what we are.

The Advaita Vedanta literature, and especially the Upanishads, await your examination and research. Can you resist this invitation of Universal Love?

What will survive of us is love.
Philip Larkin (1922–85)

Love is, above all, the gift of oneself.
Jean Anouilh

O immense Greatness! The Love-Fire rises up.
O gracious, amiable, blessed Love and clear bright
Light, tarry with us.

These words of Jakob Bohme (1575–1624) the German mystic, read by the advanced *advaita* practitioner, indicate a specific transformational stage of spiritual practice. In the final stages of duality (as the adept is realizing the One Self), the final ecstatic words of dissolving duality express the merging of *dvaita* into *a-dvaita* (Unity). Words finally cease, but it is interesting to hear the transition occurring.

Conclusion

So we approach the conclusion of this exploration of *advaita* ideas in English poetry. There are no interruptions in the continuum of poetry; this is well understood by its practitioners. James Elroy Flecker (1884–1915), an English poet and playwright who died while young, addresses a poet of 'a thousand years hence':

> O friend unseen, unborn, unknown,
>   Student of our sweet English tongue,
> Read out my words at night, alone:
>   I was a poet, I was young.
> Since I can never see your face
>   And never shake you by the hand,
> I send my soul through time and space
>   To greet you. You will understand.

The human spirit is an unchanging and everlasting principle. Whoever embodies that spirit is endowed with the power of understanding all that pertains to it without limitation of time or place.

The poet expresses the relationship between dream and reality; he interprets the reality for those who can only dream, because he glimpses it directly. This insight brings redemption to the world, held as it is in thrall to *maya* that is, to dream and illusion. The nihilistic rejection of reality comes not only from the greedy tricks of the ego's quest for instantaneous gratification, but also from the apathy of dream, and from intellectual feebleness. As the poet sifts his understanding of words, he painstakingly distils meaning from the glimpsed shapes within shadowy mystery. The poet's devotion to words is as fundamental as the potter's to the universal clay.

To change the metaphor, poetry is wondrous alchemy. It is action, passion, and power, generating and carrying the innovation that exceeds boundaries of custom and tradition. Love is at its centre, and its place is everywhere.

What of the future? The Indian poet Sri Aurobindo indicates the scale of the requirement:

> The poetry of the future has to solve
> … a problem new to the art of poetic
> speech; an utterance of the deepest
> soul of man and of the universal spirit
> of things – not only with another
> and a more complete vision, but in
> the very inmost language of the self-
> experience of the soul and the sight
> of the spiritual mind … the poets
> of whatever tongue and race who
> most completely see with this vision
> and speak with the inspiration of its
> utterance are those who shall be the
> creators of the poetry of the future.

If poetry is the ultimate expression of the human spirit, poetry offers a fresh way of learning about the meaning of Advaita Vedanta.

Kenneth Verity has worked and travelled extensively in the Far East.

He studied Zen with the Korean Master Seung Sahn, Theravāda Buddhism with Ajahn Sumedho (Thailand), and Mahayāna Buddhism with Sogyal Rinpoche (Tibet).

His understanding of Indian spiritual philosophy was deepened through absorption of the unparalleled Advaita Vedānta teachings of Shantanand Saraswatī, Shankarāchārya of Jyotir Math (India).

For many years he directed the Eastern Department of a large international arts festival near Oxford, England. He is a writer, lecturer, broadcaster, who can be heard in lectures, not infrequently, at the Nehru Centre (Indian Embassy) London.